IELTS, TOEFL, TOEIC, WAEC, NECO AND UTME

READING COMPREHENSION

WITH EXAMINATION QUESTIONS

**This book is an international passport to suc-
ceeding in all English language examination.**

**It is designed to assist learners excel
and standout in any English Language
examination (internationally or nationally).**

**It is simply educative, informative
and entertaining.**

THE OLD WOMAN
AND THE DOCTOR

An old woman, having lost the use of her eyes, called in a doctor to heal her, and made this <u>bargain</u> with him in the presence of <u>witnesses</u>: if he should cure her blindness, he would receive from her a sum of money but if her <u>infirmity</u> remained, she would give him nothing.

This agreement being made, the doctor, time after time, applied his <u>salve</u> to her eyes, and on every visit took something away, stealing all her property little by little. And when he had got all she had, he healed her and demanded the promised payment.

The old woman, when she recovered her sight saw none of her goods in the house, she gave him nothing. The doctor <u>insisted</u> on his claim and, as he still refused, <u>summoned</u> her before the judge.

The old woman, standing up in the court, argued: 'this man here speaks the truth in what he says, for I did promise to give him a sum of money if I should recover my sight, but if I remained blind, I was to give him nothing. Now he declares that I am healed. I, <u>on the contrary, affirm</u> that I am still blind; for when I lost the use of my eyes, I saw in my house various <u>chattels</u> and valuable goods. But now, though he swears I am cured of my blindness, I am not able to see a single thing in it'.

QUESTIONS

1. What bargain did the doctor make with the old woman?

2. What time did the doctor steal the old woman's property?

3. What important factor helped the doctor to steal the old woman's things?

4. What did he do when the old woman did not keep to her promise?

5. Do you think the old woman will be convicted of fraud by the judge? Why?

6. Which of the following words means the same thing as a doctor? (a) Witness (b) infirmity (c) chattels (d) physician

7. Which word in the first paragraph can replace the word agreement as used in the passage? (a) affirm (b) contrary (c) summoned (d) bargain

8. According to the passage what is the old woman's infirmity? (a) recklessness (b) courtesy (c) blindness (d) old age

9. Why did the old woman say 'I am still blind'? _________ (a) she could not find an of her property in the house. (b) she was about to be convicted by the judge. (c) she has not regained her sight. (d) the doctor did not heal her.

10. When did the doctor finally heal the old woman? (a) when she had fulfilled the bargain (b) when she had been summoned before the judge. (c) when the doctor had stolen all she had. (d) during the doctor's sixth visit.

HOMEWORK INTERRUPTED

Tabu, looked up from his book, in a lazy way at first, to see what made the noise. Then he went stiff with fright. At an arm's length away from the chair, something moved. A shape glided smoothly along the window frame. He saw a flat head held up by a slender neck. A puff adder!

The snake stopped and lay without moving. It looked dead. But all the time it was trying to sense if any food was in the room.

Tabu felt trapped in his chair, yet he knew he must warn his sister. He thought of what his father told him so often. He wanted to whisper, but his mouth and tongue were dry with shock. He dared not move. His throat clicked as he tried to utter some sound. If only she would look at him!

Masya must have felt that there was something strange about his silence, for she turned her head to glance at him. When she saw the fear on his face, she swiftly shifted round, looking at his glazed eyes. She moved her head to see what those eyes were fixed on, then covered her mouth to stifle her grasp of terror.

QUESTIONS

1. What had the snake come for?
2. Why would it stop and lie without moving?
3. What made Tabu feel trapped in his chair?
4. What effect did Tabu's fear have on him?
5. Why would he wish to warn his sister?
6. What caused Masya to look at Tabu?
7. How did she come to see where the danger was?
8. Why did she cover her mouth?
9. What do you think Tabu wanted to warn his sister to do or not to do?
10. What might have happened If Tabu had moved?

THE HISTORY OF THE YORUBA PEOPLE

The <u>ancient</u> kingdom of Ife, together with the old Oyo, <u>typified</u> some of the best examples of centralized states among the Yoruba people in the period before 1800. Ife and Oyo, together with the 'brother' kingdom of Bini, did not only share in the geographical characteristics of the forest region but also, according to tradition, had related historical roots.

Ife, regarded in some Yoruba traditions as the origin of life on earth, is also especially regarded as the father kingdom of the Yoruba people. Two <u>traditions</u> are often given to explain the origins of the Ife as a people and a kingdom. The first tradition speaks of the migration of people from the east into the present day Ile-Ife. This migrating team was said to have been led by Oduduwa who founded neighboring Yoruba towns and kingdoms. The second tradition speaks of the creation of the whole world in Ile-Ife by a <u>divine</u> order under the leadership of Obatala. However, Obatala was said to have <u>lapsed</u> in his role and the responsibility for <u>founding</u> Ife and other Yoruba towns therefore shifted into the hands of Oduduwa and fifteen others.

Though these two traditions of the origin appear to tell different stories, they nonetheless agree on two things: first, that Ife was founded and led by Oduduwa; secondly is that the Yoruba as a people <u>antedated</u> the Oduduwa period. In attempting to <u>reconcile</u> both traditions, it has been argued that the tradition of Oduduwa need not necessarily be interpreted to mean the origin of a people, but perhaps, the <u>demise</u> of one <u>epoch</u> in the history of the Yoruba people (possibly the Obatala period) and the <u>commencement</u> of another (the Oduduwa period).

QUESTIONS

1. Which kingdom is considered as being very close to the Yoruba kingdoms of Ife and Oyo?

2. How many traditions are often cited to explain the origin of the Yoruba people?

3. Which kingdom is regarded as the father of all the Yoruba kingdoms?

3. Which two important personalities are linked to the creation of the Yoruba race?

4. Who founded Yoruba towns and villages apart from Ife?

5. Which one of the following shares the same origin with the Yoruba people? (a) Tiv kingdom (b) Ijaw kingdom (c) Bini kingdom (d) Obatala kingdom

6. The word <u>antedated</u> as used in the third paragraph means _____. (a) went behind (b) occurred before (c) came later than (d) came after a problem.

7. The passage seems to suggest that _______. (a) Oduduwa appeared before Obatala. (b) Obatala appeared before Oduduwa. (c) Oduduwa fought Obatala to found Ife. (d) Obatala forces Oduduwa to leave Ife.

8. Which one of the following words is a simple present tense form of <u>founding</u> as used in the second paragraph? (a) find (b) found (c) fond (d) fend

9. Which one of the following has the same meaning as the word <u>divine</u> (adj) as used in the second paragraph? (a) earthly (b) satanic (c) dive (d) heavenly

THE LONG TREK

Steve reckoned that they were about three miles from the river, if there was still a river. By now, it might be just a trickle of slow-moving water, or a bed of dried mud, full of tumbleweed and stones.

He closed his eyes to slits as he peered through the clouds of dust –red dust kicked up by hundreds of hoofs. The cattle that streamed past him as he sat slumped in his saddle were as tired and worn-out as the exhausted men who drove them.

Some of them bellowed with fear and pain. The calves pushed their noses into the side of the cows that had no milk to feed them. All of them were mad with thirst and very thin. From their knob-like backbones, the drawn skin was tight over the fleshless haunches. Their ribs curved like the bars of a cage over their sunken flanks. They were starving.

They had trekked from the cattle stations in the north of Australia where usually heavy rains filled streams and pools. But this was a year of drought. The burning sun, which had sucked up the last drop of water, had left the ground cracked and dry. Wide, dangerous ruts had formed in the earth. They were deep and broad enough to wedge a man's boot when he walked. There was only one thing to do. The cattle must be driven many miles south, to the river; or they would die.

QUESTIONS

1. Why did Steve sit "slumped" in his addle?
2. What did he fear might have happened to the river?
3. Why were the animals' backbones like knobs?
4. What other effects had the drought on them?
5. What is a drought?
6. Why would the ground have cracks?
7. Had the sun really "sucked" up drops of water?
8. Why where the ruts in the earth dangerous?
8. If the river was dry, what then?
9. What effects would a drought have in your area?

MONDAY MORNING

Monday morning found Tom Sawyer miserable. Monday morning always found him so, because it began another week's slow suffering in school. He generally began that day with wishing he had had no intervening holiday; it made the going into captivity and chains again so much more odious.

Tom lay thinking. Presently it occurred to him that he wished he was sick; then he could stay at home from school. Here was a vague possibility. He canvassed his system. No ailment was found, and he investigated again. This time he thought he could detect colicky symptoms, and he began to encourage them with considerable hope. But they soon grew feeble and presently died away. He reflected further. Suddenly he discovered something. One of his upper teeth was loose. This was lucky; he was about to groan, as a "starter", as he called it, when it occurred to him that if he came into court with that argument his aunt would pull it out, and that would hurt. So, he thought he would hold the tooth in reverse for the present and seek further. Nothing offered for some little time, and then he remembered hearing the doctor telling about a certain thing that laid up a patient for two or three weeks and threatened to make him lose a finger. So, the boy eagerly drew his sore toe from under the sheet and held it up for inspection. But now he did not know the necessary symptoms. However, it seemed well worthwhile to chance it, so he fell to groaning with considerable spirit.

QUESTIONS

1. Where was Tom when he was doing his thinking?
2. What prospect was making him miserable?
3. What was the purpose of his thinking?
4. What three ideas did he have for achieving his purpose?
5. hat caused him to reject his first idea?
6. Why did he not adopt his second idea?
7. What is meant by holding a tooth "in reverse"?
8. What is the difference between a symptom and an ailment?

THE FOX

The fox is probably the most intelligent of all quadrupeds. It is allied to the dog and closely resembles the Alsatian, the wolf, the hyena, the coyote (prairie-wolf of North America), the dingo (native dog of Australia), and the dhole (wild dog of India). Its chief point of difference from the others are the sharper muzzle and the shorter legs in proportion to the size of the body. Its tail or "brush" is also longer, and its ears more erect.

The fox has eyes with pupils that contract in strong light and expand in darkness. This enables the animal to hunt at night. It excavates its own lair by burrowing much like a rabbit, but frequently it is a thief in this respect as it steals burrows from other animals and converts them into its own "earth". The cunning and slyness of the animal is shown by the number of exits to its lair. As many as ten bolt-holes from the fox's "earth" have been counted. Its power of scent is very acute, and its hearing very highly developed. The animal has a peculiar strong scent, which leaves the "trail" in the so-called sport of fox-hunting. When the chase is keen Reynard frequently escapes by dashing into wide and open drainpipes. For this reason, one may see gratings placed over the mouths of many roadside and field drains. When cornered by the hounds the animal has been known to climb roofs of houses and to dash into nearby cottages in desperate efforts to shake off its pursuers.

QUESTIONS

1. What two words are used for the fox's den?

2. What special name is sometimes given to a fox?

3. What animal does the fox resemble when digging?

4. What enables the hound to track down the fox?

5. Give two reasons why the fox is a difficult animal to catch.

6. Name any other creature which hunts at night.

7. Give two points of difference between the fox and the dog.

THE TWIN

The twin grew tall and strong like plantain trees. Ngozi was like her mother, gentle and soft-spoken. Emeka was like his father, strong and self-willed.

Sometimes their mother took them to town to see their aunt. Their aunt sold cloth in the market and she was very fond of the twins. She bought them clothes and biscuits. Ngozi loved biscuits, and she always took some back to the farm with her for the other children.

Emeka did not like the town very much. He was a farm boy. He loved the farm. He worked with his father on the farm. He helped him to clear the bushes around the yams and he helped him with the sticks which were used to hold up the tendrils. He enjoyed working with his father. But he preferred fishing and hunting. Like his father, he was a good fisherman. He loved fishing with other children. Ngozi was not good at fishing. She always caught very few fish. Emeka caught plenty. All the other children on the farm had catapults and, one day, Emeka's father bought a catapult for his son too. Early in the morning as soon as they had eaten, they all went out to shoot lizards. This was a wonderful game. When Emeka shot more lizards than the other boys, he was very happy.

Then, one day when the twins were nine years old, they went to live with their aunt in town. Their aunt was very pleased to see them. When the twins arrived, the first thing she did was to make new clothes for them. Emeka was not very interested in the new clothes. He wanted to go back home to the farm where he could hunt lizards with the other children. But Ngozi was pleased with her new clothes and she liked living with her aunt. In the mornings they went to the stream to fetch water. When they came back they had breakfast. Then they carried the boxes of cloth to the market for their aunt. Ngozi stayed in the market all day and helped her aunt. Emeka went fishing and hunting, just as he had done on the farm.

QUESTIONS

1. Who did the twins look like?

2. Where did the twins sometimes go?

3. What did Ngozi enjoy doing?

4. Why did Ngozi enjoy those activities?

5. What did Emeka prefer doing?

6. Why did Emeka enjoy his own activities?

7. did Emeka enjoy doing?

8. Who did the twins help?

9. Why did Emeka not like the town?

10. Where the twins alike?

MY FIRST DAY AT SECONDARY SCHOOL

My name is John. My first day at Hope secondary was an eventful one. As it is natural for every student to remember the first day at school, I can remember vividly the things that happened. It was my father who prepared the way for my admission to the school. He collected the admission form and my mother filled them in. I wrote the entrance examination some four weeks afterwards. The results were released and my name was first on the list of successful candidates. My sisters and my parents were very happy.

Hope secondary was sold and well- known school in my locality. It had gigantic buildings with large compound built with beautiful well-arranged flowers.

When I stepped into the school first I felt nervous at first because of the large crowd of people swarming around on the first day. Most parents mostly mothers, accompanied their children to school. My father accompanied me that day because my mother had travelled away. The atmosphere of the school was bustling and full of life as a lot of new and returning students were busy with one thing or another. Teacher after teacher went to different classes.

When I had enrolled as a student, I went to my class. The class teacher, Mrs. Kofo Adebola asked my name, home address and age. I answered her question quickly. She was impressed, so she patted me on my back. Her kind behavior soothed my feelings. Other students in class looked at me curiously. After two conservative periods there was a recess of 15 minutes. I dashed to the playground with my classmates. I made friends with Chinedu, Adeola and Ahmed. We told stories of our primary school days. My initial anxiety vanished because of my friends.

Soon the bell rang for us to go home after the eight periods. Many students were relieved to be with their parents again. I was delighted to see my father waiting for me at the school gate. My first day at school is pleasant to recollect.

QUESTIONS

1. Why was john nervous on the first day at school?

2. Why did John's mother not accompany him to school?

3. What other word can be used to replace *natural* in the first paragraph?

4. Why was John's first day at school an eventful one?

5. What affected John's feelings?

From 6-10 just write down the option of the right answer.

6. Which word in the passage means the same as disappeared? (a) consecutive (b) patted (c) vanished (d) soothed

7. Which one of the following is true about John's first day at school?

PATRIOTISM

Patriotism is how we show our love and our readiness to serve our country. If we are patriotic, we must be loyal to our country and not our ethnic group. Patriots must speak well of their country at all times. If patriots are outside their country, they must not say or do anything that will harm the country, even if they are not happy with the government.

If Nigerians are called to serve Nigeria in any way, either in time of peace or war, they should be ready to serve. If there had been no patriotism on the part of the Nigerian armed forces, Nigeria would not exist today as she does. A patriotic person must place the country above the state or ethnic group.

As a citizen of Nigeria, we should be loyal to our governments-state and federal. We should pay our taxes, defend our nation at all times, show respect for our leaders and all national symbols, be honest in all our dealing with fellow citizens and, above all, keep and defend the constitution or laws of the nation.

Being a good citizen also means respect for national identity. That is, a patriotic citizen respects the symbols of a nation, those things by which a nation is known or identified. The main symbols of a nation are the national anthem, the national flag, the national pledge, the armed forces, the coat of arms, a single currency, common boundaries and cultural artifacts, as well as the language we speak and the way we dress, which identify us as Nigerians. Respect for national identity gives us a sense of unity. If we are not loyal to our country, we will not even know if Nigeria's enemies are planning to attack the country. There is a saying that if you call your own calabash a useless one, other people will use it as a refuse bin. So if you do not love your country, other people may do anything to it without your knowledge.

QUESTION

1. How does the author describe patriotism in the passage?

2. Mention two things a patriot must not do outside the country.

3. Mention one organ of the government that saved Nigeria from division.

4. What things do you think are referred to as

artifacts in the passage?

5. The writer equates being a good citizen with one thing in the last paragraph. What is it?

From number 6-10 write the option with the right answer.

6. Which of the following is true of patriots?

(a) They always show an uncaring attitude to their country

(b) They allow ethnic interest to rule their minds

(c) They are always ready to serve in times of peace and war

(d) They are loyal to their country only in times of peace

7. The primary purpose of this passage is to

    a. Encourage Nigerians to be loyal in their country

    b. Describe the role of the Nigerian armed forces

    c. Explain how many cultural artifact Nigeria has

    d. Inform us of what constitute human right

8. According to the passage , patriots should be

loyal even if

    a.They are pleased with the situation of the country

    b. They are not pleased with the country

    c. They are from a minority ethnic group

    d. The laws of the constitution are broken

9. According to the passage, which of this is a consequence of lack of loyalty to one's country?

    a. Cultural artifacts will be destroyed

    b. Enemies can easily attack the country

    c. National symbols can be stolen

    d. The national budget will be affected as a result of non- payment taxes

10. Which of the following is the highest form of patriotism according to the passage?

    a. rotecting cultural artifacts

    b. payment of taxes

    c. serving in the armed forces

    d. defending the constitution

A WONDERFUL NEW WORLD

At school, I found myself in a new and wonderful world. For the first time I saw a laboratory and we started to learn some real science. To begin with, I was completely puzzled by the biology classes but soon the subject came to have a great fascination for me. I had never been in mathematics but at Munali I had a good teacher and the subject soon lost it terror so that when we took the final examinations I came second in the class. History had always been my best subject but for some reasons I did not do well in it, perhaps because it was all South African history that we study. English literature I came to love but I did badly in the grammar paper at the end of my course.

We lived a full and interesting life at Munali. It was by no means all work and study in the classroom. I immediately found myself in the football team and we had many exciting and some very rough matches with local teams. I still carry on my leg a large scar, where I was injured by the boot of one of the Lusaka "Tigers". Great emphasis was laid on athletics and I ran for my house in the mile and half- mile. In my second year, I led my house to victory in the interhouse athletics competition although I nearly caused my house to lose the cup by my performance in the mile race. I led the field in the first and second laps but I must have started out at first too fast a pace because I was soon lagging far behind. Even though I was last, I ran the race to the end and I received the house trophy, the principal commended me.

During my second year, I was captain of my house with a small room to myself at the end of the dormitory. Many of the younger boys in the in the first year would come and hide in my room when ragging was in progress, and I did all I could to protect them and discouraged any form of bullying in my dormitory. I had learnt the value of strict discipline from my parents and was determined to have the same kind of discipline in the school during the week I was duty prefect. The boys soon discovered that during my week on duty there were no detentions to be worked off on Saturday. I also became quite popular with the housemaster and teacher who rarely had to punish anyone during my duty period.

QUESTIONS

Now read the questions carefully. They require answers that begin with 'yes' or 'no'. but you are required to give reason alongside your answer.

1. Did the writer enjoy life at secondary school?

2. Did he do well in his science subjects?

3. Did he do well in history?

4. Did he go to classes only?

5. Did he play on the football team?

6. Did he win the mile race?

7. Did he win a trophy for himself?

8. Did he put up with bullying in his dormitory?

9. Did the boys and masters like him?

10. Did he show the qualities of a leader even as aboy?

FLOWERS

When a bee or an ant, a beetle or butterfly visit a flower for food, it simultaneously and without knowing it, performs another vital function as it carries pollen from one plant to another. The flowers they visit depend on those insects to ensure the continuity of their existence. However, it is not all flowers that the ant or bee or moth or beetle or butterfly visits. Only those flowers that are attractive, showy and flamboyant enjoy the visitation. Plants thus, use their large, colourful and sweet smell to entice insects.

What about grass flower then? Does grass have flowers? Yes, it does. The flowers are graceful but not flamboyant and therefore, grass flowers do not interest the bee or ant or beetle or moth or butterfly. In this case, pollen is carried by the wind. Most flowers manufacture these minute grains called pollen which must be transferred to another flower of the same type before they can make seeds.   A single flower can produce fifty million of them.

QUESTIONS

1. What is the main reason why a bee or moth or butterfly visits flowers? It _______ (a) Enjoys the sweet smell of the flowers (b) goes there to mate. (c) Goes there to obtain food. (d) Carries pollen from the flowers.

2. What is one general name given to bees, beetles, moths and butterflies? (a) animals (b) insects (c) pollinators (d) pollen carriers

3. What other function does the bee or ant or moth perform apart from the main one when it visits flowers? It _____________. (a) Carries pollen from one plant to another. (b) Enjoys itself. (c) Ensure the continuity of plants. (d) Produces pollen.

4. Which of the flower does the bee or moth or ant visit? It visits the ones that______. (a) are grassy (b) have pollen (c) are flowery (d) are attractive, showy and flamboyant

5. Why does the bee or ant or butterfly not visit grass flowers? It is because they are______. (a) Not showy and flamboyant. (b) Graceful. (c) Little flowers (d) grassy.

6. How can seeds be made by flowers? Seeds can be made by _________. (a) The production of pol-

len. (b) Transferring pollens from one flower to another of the same type. (c) The flamboyance of flowers. (d) The beautiful colours of flowers.

7. What is the effect of a bee or a butterfly or ant carrying pollen from one flower to another? (a) It makes it possible to produce seeds. (b) Much food is produced for it. (c) It makes it possible for a flower to produce 50 million flowers. (d) It is kept busy.

8. The last sentence states 'a single flower can produce fifty million of them' fifty millions of what? (a) flowers (b) plants (c) seeds (d) pollen

9. According to the passage, a bee or moth or butterfly or an ant carries pollen from one flower to another___________. (a)unconsciously (b) regularly (c) knowingly (d) as a vital function

For each of the following words give another word or phrase that means the same and can replace the word as it used in the passage:

Manufacture

Vital

THE MOSQUITO
AND THE EAR

The entire world was starving. There was hardly a morsel of food left anywhere. Only the mosquito had a little calabash bowl of flour hidden away. Each day the mosquito mixed a bit of porridge and carefully hid the remainder under a stone, in the corner of his hut. The ear was starving and in desperation came to seek for food at the mosquito's house.

He was so lean he could hardly walk. As he approached the mosquito's house, he saw him hide something under a stone.

When the mosquito had gone to bathe in the river, the ear stole the bowl of flour and made a big dish of porridge and shares it with its hundreds of hungry children.

The mosquito returned from his bath and was hungry, so he looked under the stone to get some flour and found that it was gone. He quickly flew to his nearest neighbor, the ear and demanded for his food.

"If you don't give me back my flour, I shall never leave you. I will bother you when you hunt or fish or sleep", whined the mosquito comes to bite a man, the chief of all living things, it first goes to the ear and whines, "Give me my flour".

If ear hears it and does not give it, the mosquito takes his food where he can find it.

QUESTIONS

According to the passage, what was the condition of entire world when the story was narrated?

1. What did mosquito do in order to save himself from starvation?

2. Why did the ear pay the mosquito a visit?

3. According to the passage, what was the condition of the ear as he was going to mosquito's house?

4. Who is the chief of all living things according to the passage?

5. Where was the mosquito when the ear stole his flour?

6. What was the decision of the mosquito if the ear failed to return his flour?

7. "If you don't give me back my flour, I shall

never leave you" What type of adverbial clause is this?

8. State the synonym s for these words: morsel, approached.

9. Suggest a suitable title for this passage.

GREEDY ROBBERS

Three <u>highway</u> robbers, Kalou, Zidane and Ye-kini, once hid under the Eko Bridge to wait for <u>passersby</u> who they could rob. Week after week, they had <u>seized</u>travellers' belongings. Kalou was the eldest and Yekini the young-est. All were armed with pistols and daggers.

One day, a well-dressed man <u>approached</u> the bridge. From his appearance, the robbers <u>con-cluded</u> that he had plenty of money. They de-cided to attack and rob him.

When the traveller reached the middle of the bridge, Kalou<u>commanded</u> him to stop and sur-render himself to be searched. The other fired several shots into the air to frighten him. From the traveller's pockets, the robbers got five thou-sand naira. Then, they let him go free because he had obeyed their command.

The robbers met the following day to share the money. Yekini was given five hundred naira to buy them some breakfast. When he had left, the others planned to kill him on his return and share the money between the two of them. On the way, Yekini also made up his mind to take all the money. To do this, he put a <u>deadly</u> poison in the food so that the other two would eat it and die.

As soon as he came back, they <u>sprang</u> on him, killed him and started to enjoy their food. But before very long, they started to vomit and soon they too were dead.

QUESTIONS

1. How much did the robbers get from the traveller's pockets?

2. Who ordered the traveller to stop?

3. How did the robbers know that the traveller had a lot of money?

4. Who were the people who fired shots into the air?

5. What happened to Kalou and Zidane after they ate the food?

6. Which of the robbers held pistols and daggers? (a) Kalou and Zidane (b) Zidane and Yekini (c) Kalou, Yekini and Zidane (d) Kalou only

7. What was the first thing Kalou and Zidane did

after Yekini brought the food? (a) They ate the food (b) they jumped on him (c) they vomited (d) they committed suicide

8. What important moral lesson can we learn from this passage? (a) That we should not be greedy (b) that we could be selfish sometimes (c) that people should not kill their friends (d) that robbery can lead to death.

9. Another word that can replace <u>approached</u> as used in the passage is (a) Moved away from (b) saw (c) moved towards (d) moved under

10. The word <u>deadly</u> as used in the paragraph means (a) Mild (b) moderate (c) causing sleep (d) causing death.

GOAL

One day my friends – Tomi – asked me a question when I was in JS Two. The question was, 'Do you have a goal?' my reply was that I had one and it was to excel in my promotion examination. 'That is good but it is a short term one,' he replied. 'What exactly do you want to become?' he asked further. 'I am too young for that; I can become anything – a doctor, an engineer, a banker, a lawyer, just anything. 'I replied and I added, 'when I get to SS Three I will think about it.'

Tomi then took time to enlighten me: 'listen Jumai, don't deceive yourself, you must have a <u>particular</u> goal. Do you want to become a member of the NFA? You know NFA? No Future Ambition. You have to think of what you want to become right now so that you can study towards it. You just don't wake up one day to become a doctor, lawyer. What you want to become requires careful planning. For instance, your goal will determine the type of subjects you are going to combine. You will not just combine any subject with any other one. You need to combine the relevant subject that will lead to your course of study. If for an example you want to be an engineer, apart from concentrating on English language and mathematics, you need to devote much attention to basic science and technology. These subjects will help you when you get to the senior secondary school where you will study physics, chemistry and technical drawing among other subjects.

'I see, but how did you <u>obtain</u> this <u>vital</u> information? Jumai asked, 'my father happens to be a Guidance and Counsellor and he has explained everything about the choice of a career to me. Don't you have a guidance and counsellor in your school? If you do, go directly to him or her and he or she will <u>counsel</u> you?

'So, what is your own goal?' I asked. I want to be a dentist. I will soon be helping you and other people to take <u>adequate</u> care of their teeth. I will read dentistry at the university.' Tomi replied.

'Thank you, Tomi, you have really enlightened me today. I will go straight to our school's Guidance and counsellor, 'I concluded.

QUESTIONS

1. What does it mean to have 'a goal' as it is used in the passage?

2. What was the immediate goal of Jumai?

3. When did Jumai want to think about what she wanted to become?

4. Why did Jumai need to think about her goal in JS Two that she was?

5. What would determine one's subject combination?

6. How did Tomi have such information on having a goal?

7. What was the profession of Tomi's father?

8. What work do Guidance counsellors do according to the passage?

9. Who is a dentist?

10. What is the writer's purpose in this passage?

EVOLUTION OF MONEY

The evolution of money can be traced back to the time of the early man, who lived <u>subsistence</u> life. As the society grew, his wants became numerous. So he needed the goods and service produced by others to satisfy his basics needs. <u>This gave rise to</u> the barter system of exchange. This was a situation whereby goods and services were exchanged for other goods and services. It clearly marked the beginning of commerce.

In the barter system, different products were exchanged for other products at various times. Some difficulties were associated with the barter system. The difficulties included double <u>coincidence</u> of wants. For example, yams were exchanged for goats, fish for logs, even gin or rum for human beings, as it helps during the slave trade <u>era</u>. Other problems have to do with storage and transportation issues.

<u>Later</u> development saw different commodities being used as money, until the barter system

collapsed, and was therefore abandoned. Some of the commodities used for exchange were beads, tobacco, salt, seeds, manila, metal, cowries, shells, precious feathers, textile materials, as well as cows. The commodities exchanged were also relatively scarce, which made them valuable and acceptable. Internal and external trade also determined the commodity to be used for exchange.

In Nigeria, the use of metal coins and paper money started before the colonization of Nigeria by the British Government. The currencies of some European countries such as Spain, France, and Portugal were in circulation in Nigeria. Their currencies were withdrawn and replaced by legal tender put into circulation by the West African Currency Board, which was established by the British government in 1912. Prior to the attainment of independence, the Central Bank of Nigeria was established precisely on July 1, 1959, to commence the issuance of currencies and notes as legal tender.

QUESTION

1. What type of life did the early man live?

2. What gave rise to the barter system of exchange?

3. one major difficulty with the barter system.

4. Why were the commodities exchanged under the barter system valuable and acceptable?

5. Which bank issues currencies as legal tender?

6. What part of speech is the word 'issuance' as used in the last paragraph?

(a) Noun (b) verb (c) adverb (d) adjectives

7. Which of these is not true about the barter system of exchange?

8. The barter system of exchange happened when man's wants became numerous. (b) Barter involves exchange of goods and services. (c) Some difficulties were associated with the barter exchange system. (d) War gave rise to the barter exchange system.

9. Another word that can replace evolution as used in the passage is _________. (a) Revolution (b) resolution (c) solution (d) growth

10. Which of the following was NOT mentioned among the commodities used as money under the barter system of exchange?

(a) Precious feather (b) tobacco (c) cows (d) horses

11. When did the use of paper money start in

Nigeria?

Before colonisation (b) after colonisation (c) during colonisation (d) in 1973

THE BLOOD

Blood, which the heart pumps round the body, is necessary to the life of every person. If the heart stops pumping (and nothing replaces it) then the person will die. The pumping may be stopped for a short period, but not too long enough for surgeons to perform any difficult operation.

For example, the brain is likely to die if we stop the flow of blood for longer than three minutes at the body's normal temperature, and this is not long enough for most operations. How then can surgeons perform operations on the heart? One answer is to lower the temperature from 38centigrate to 30centigrate. This is long enough for certain operations.

We can also stop the supply of blood to the brain for as long as an hour by taking the temperature of the body down to below 15centigrate. There are however, a number of dangers in thus method especially as the patient is almost certainly weak from illness before the operation.

QUESTION

1. What is the major idea in the first paragraph?

(a) The function of blood (b) pumping of blood (c) the activities of the human heart (d) the importance of the human heart

2. The first paragraph implies that

(a) Blood is required for difficult operations. (b) Blood is necessary to the life of everybody. (c) The functioning of the heart may not be stopped at all. (d) The heart itself moves round the body to perform its functions.

3. Which of the following options best sums up the function of the heart?

(a) The heart pumps blood to the body. (b) It supplies blood to every part of the brain. (c) It supplies blood to the body only during operation. (d) It stops the flow of blood when the temperature is high.

4. Identify one major idea in the second paragraph.

(a) There is a link between the heart and the flow of the blood. (b) Surgeons can perform operations if there is blood supply. (c) The body temperature required to perform an operation is between 30centigrate to 38centigrate. (d) An operation cannot be performed in ten minutes.

5. The key idea in paragraph three is that ;

(a) There is no limit to which the body temperature. (b) Supply of blood to the brain can be lowered for at least on hour. (c) Many patients have body temperature of below 15centigrates. (d) There is no danger in reducing body temperature at 15centigrates.

6. It is deduced from the passage that at the point of operation is always

(a) Agile and well fed. (b) Afraid and nervous. (c) Allowed to recover from illness. (d) Weak from illness.

7. Paragraph three states that stopping blood supply to the brain for as long as one hour is

A dangerous operation. (b) The safest method of operation. (c) a very mild operation (d) possible only in adults.

8. A suitable title for the passage could be

(a) The problems of surgeons (b) human body temperature (c) danger of performing operation (d) how to reduce body temperature

9. The passage leads us to conclude that ....

(a) Surgeons cannot perform operations at all

(b) an operation can be performed on the heart when the body temperature is lowered. (c) Surgeons can stop the flow of blood to the brain when the temperature is above 38centigrate (d) the brain is likely to die if the blood flow is stopped for one minute.

10. From the passage, we conclude that

Nothing can replace the heart. (b) There is danger in lowering the body temperature below a certain level (c) the brain is alive even when the heart stops functioning for two hours (d) the heart manufactures blood.

BRIBERY AND CORRUPTION

Bribery and corruption have continued to remain in our society as an <u>insurmountable social</u> evil. Some people are of the opinion that they have come to stay as part of our culture. Right from the village square, among the <u>rural</u> community, to the seat of power in government, there are obvious signs and instances of bribery and corruption.

For example, a politician who has gone to the rural areas to <u>canvass</u> for votes during elections has not started if he begins to address the villager without first presenting <u>kola.</u> Besides, he would be expected to <u>beam</u> his torchlight to <u>demonstrate</u> his seriousness. The rural dwellers argue that that is the only way to get their share of the <u>national</u> cake their democracy <u>dividends.</u> Are they right? The 'ten per cent' has become an official jargon among those who deal in contracts within private and public agencies, ministries and local governments.

Similarly, educational institutions are not left out. Lecturers print handouts and students are expected to buy them at fixed prices and if they refuse, they face the consequences. On a more serious note, there have been cases in which rich students give lecturers gifts in cash during festivals and, in turn, they are <u>considered</u> when the moment comes.

There have been instances of sexual <u>harassment</u> by lecturers to female students in higher institutions. All these and more constitute corruption.

The <u>monster</u> is national social evil and will remain a <u>menace</u> in our national life. Opinions tend to the general agreement that the evil must be fought from the top. The cleansing must start from top leaders in government, executives and agencies. The approach by the government should be <u>decisive</u> and total and not <u>selective</u>. Anything short of this amounts to not hitting the nail on the head.

QUESTIONS

1. Mention two groups identified by the writer as agents of bribery and corruption.

2. What do you think the writer means by <u>kola</u> in the second paragraph?

3. What type of corruption is said to be common among university lecturers?

4. What does the writer refer to as 'the monster' in the last paragraph?

5. What should the government do in order to hit the nail of corruption on the head?

5. Why is corruption 'a menace' in our national life? Because
   (a) Everybody hates corruption. (b) Some people embrace bribery while hating corruption. (c) Corruption is a great danger to the country as a whole. (d) Some people like corruption while they still complain.
6. According to the writer, efforts at stopping corruption should start with…
   (a) The public (b) the civil service (c) the military (d) the government officials and agencies
7. The tone of the passage could be described as ……
   Satirical (b) sarcastic (c) objective (d) suspicious
8. What does the word <u>they</u> refer to as used in line 4 in the first paragraph?
   (a) Bribery and corruption (b) rural community (c) politicians (d) some people in government.

9. The word <u>canvass</u>as used in the second paragraph means.
  (a) Confuse (b) persuade (c) dissuade (d) reveal

THE PYGMIES AND THEIR PRISONER

Long ago, the ship of an English sailor sank in the Atlantic Ocean near Africa. All the people in the ship except the sailor drowned in the storm.

The waves threw him upon the shores of the continent. When he came to himself he travelled inland until he reached the land of the pygmies. The size and the appearance of these people surprised the sailors for he had never seen such human beings before.

The pygmies who lived in the heart of the Congo basin are the shortest people in the world. Their average height is three feet four inches. The king of the pygmies ordered some of his officers to search the prisoner's belongings.

Inside one of the sailor's pocket, they found a watch fastened with a chain. The officers were so afraid of this object that they refused to handle it. Some thought that the small animals the sailors had tamed were making the noise inside the watch. Others thought that I might be a kind of god that he worshipped.

Questions

1. Where did the ship sink?

2. ho was safe after the shipwreck?

3. Where was the sailor thrown?

4. What people did he see?

5. Why was he surprised?

6. Where did these people lie?

7. What were the officers ordered to do?

8. What did they find in his pocket?

9. Why were they officer afraid?

10. What did they think?

THE VILLAGE ANT HILL

In the centre of Mbeke village is the old ant-hill. School children often go to this city of ants to study insects.

An ant is a good example of an insect, for its body has three divisions-the head, the thorax and the abdomen, with six legs.

Ant cities are made of earth and many are built under ground. The village ant-hill is above the surface and is over two meters high. Ants move in and out of their home through many holes in this ant-hill.

Like human beings, ants live together in cities where work is done in groups. The soldiers defend the city. The soldiers have bigger heads than the others. Another group has the duty of keeping the city clean. Ants are very tidy little creatures. They allow no dirt or food to remain inside or near their homes.   Others hunt for food in groups; they drag heavy bits of food into the ant-hill. Little bits are carried home in their mouths. They march like an army of soldiers over the grass, over the rubbish heaps and any-where in search of food.

The nurse-ants look after the baby ones. Those wounded during accidents are well cared for too. In fact, ants, like bees, are very wonderful and interesting little crea-tures. They live together and help one an-other.

Questions

1. Where is the village ant-hill?

2. Why do children go there?

3. Name the body divisions of an art.

4. What is this ant-hill made of?

5. How high is it?

6. What class defends the city?

7. do ants search for food?

8. Which class cares for the
babies and the wounded?

9. What other creature is like the ant?

10. In what ways are ants
like human beings?

FAMILY

A nuclear family is a group consisting of a father, mother and children, who share living quarters. The opposite of the nuclear family is the extended family which apart from the people in the nuclear family also comprises other relatives such as uncles, aunts, cousins and nephew. Nuclear family structure dates back thousands of years. In its general meaning, the term nuclear refers to a central entity or nucleus around which others collect.

According to Professor Wolfgang Haak of Adelaide University, the nuclear family is natural to Homo sapiens (the present generation of the human species). A 2005 archeological dig in Elan, Germany, analyzed Haak, revealed genetic evidence suggesting that the individuals found in a grave were closely related. Haak said, 'By establishing the genetic links between the two adults and two children buried together in one grave, we have established the presence of the classic nuclear family in a <u>prehistoric</u> context in central Europe. 'Most modern western cultures are <u>dominated</u> by the nuclear family mentality.

The term extended, family has been generally used to refer to grandparent, uncles, aunts and cousins, whether they live together within the same <u>household</u> or not. It may also refer to a family unit together within a single household. In India, the family is a <u>patriarchal</u> rather than a <u>matriarchal</u> society, with the sons' families often staying under a single roof. In this kind of set up, work is shared among the members, often unequally. The women are often housewives and cook for the entire family. The patriarch of the family (often the oldest male member) lays down the rules and judges dispute. Other senior members of the household baby-sit infants when their mothers are working. They are also responsible for teaching the younger children their mother tongue, manner and etiquette.

Most extended family houses often have large reception area and a common kitchen. Each family has its own bedroom. The members of the household also look after one another if a member is ill.

QUESTIONS:

1. are the members of the nuclear family?

2. In one sentence describe the nuclear family.

3. Which type of family has the grandmother as a member?

4. What is the name of the current generation of human beings mentioned in the passage?

5. What does the word *baby-sit* mean?

6. In which of the following cultures

is the family system dominated by the nuclear family mentality?

7. Which of the family is not a member of the nuclear family?

(a) father (b) son (c) cousin (d) mother

8. Which family leadership system exists in India?

(a) Matriarchal (b) patriarchal (c) homo-sapiens (d) species

9. The word 'prehistoric' in the second paragraph means___

(a) After written history (b) before written history (c) immediately after written history (d) after the age of the dinosaurs.

10. Which of the following is true of an extended family?

(a) Western cultures are always domin-ated by the extended family system. (b) Extended family members never live to-gether. (c) Some extended family member may or may not stay in the same quarters. (d) in India, the oldest family becomes the head of the family.

COMMUNICATION

Learning to speak one's language comes naturally to a human being; we learn it without formal instruction. But writing is an unnatural activity; it must be taught formally and studied _deliberately_. Indeed, many of the problems that arise in learning to write are simply problems of finding proper written equivalent for the various features of speech. The spelling of our words is a clumsy attempt to produce the sound of our voices. The punctuation of our sentences and the setting of paragraphs are _designed_ to give some approximation of the pauses and the intonation we use automatically to give shape and point to our speaking.

The writer of English (or any other language) loses a whole world of gestures, facial expressions and tone of voices the minute he decides to write something rather than say it aloud. He loses the immediacy of direct contact with his audience. If there were no _compensation_ at all for all these advantages, then communicating with other people through the medium of squiggles on paper would be as unsatisfactory as trying to wash your feet with your socks on.

Writing takes more effort than speech, but the effort we make simply to capture our words with paper can also lead us to compose things that are worth the effort. The unusual energy that goes into achievement in any art or sport can and should function finally to help the individual increase his own power and his abilities. Three hundred and fifty years ago, a clever man pointed out that practice in speaking makes a man ready or quick in his responses, while practice in writing makes a man "exact", helps him to polish and perfect thoughts.

QUESTIONS

1. Why did the writer say that writing is an unnatural activity?

2. Give two specific examples of problems encountered in learning to write.

3. Mention any two disadvantages that arise in written communication.

4. What major advantage comes from acquisition of good writing skills?

5. .... that goes into achievement in any art or sport

    I What grammatical name is used to describe the above expression?

    II What is its function?

6. For each of the following, find another word or phrase that means the same and can replace is as used in the passage.

    Deliberately

    Equivalent

    Designed

    Compensation

ANGER

It was the occasion of the annual prize giving ceremony in our school. Taiwo wanted to appear unique and different from other students. So he wore his baggy pants to school.

As soon as he appeared, his classmates began to hail him-'Tai-Tai-Tai-Tai in trousers' he himself was beaming with smiles. Everybody laughed and their ribs were nearly cracking. As he moved closer to the venue of the ceremony – Obedience Hall-the shout of' Tai-tai-tai' became louder. His baggy pants were flapping round his legs. One of his classmates Dankoro 'Karo' for short approached him and began to flip one leg of the baggy trouser which was enough for two people to enter into.

At this point, the fun grew sour as Taiwo felt enraged and punched Dakoro in the face. Blood began to gush out of his mouth and soon the beautifully embroidered dress became blood-soaked. Many of his classmates took to their heels but few stayed to take care of Dakoro. Incidentally as the principal was accompanying one of the guests to his office, he noticed the unusual gathering. He took an excuse from his guest and found what had happened. He immediately ordered Dakoro to be taken to the hospital for proper treatment.

The ceremony started as planned and all the activities on the programme were carried out. Prizes were given to students who excelled in academics, morals and appearance. Unknown to him, Taiwo was slated to receive the two best prizes for his outstanding academic performance and for being the best-behaved student throughout the session.

When it got to his turn, the principal made the following announcements: 'The two best prizes for the best-all round student in academics and the best behaved student. Unfortunately, an incident occurred this morning and because of this incident the winner of the prizes, Taiwo peace who exhibited some form of violence during the incident will no longer receive them. 'Taiwo was shocked as soon as he heard this and broke down in tear.

QUESTIONS

1. For what occasion did Taiwo
wear baggy pants?

2. Where did the occasion take place?

3. ow often was the occasion
usually celebrated?

4. How did the principal get to
know of the incident?

5. Why did Taiwo wear baggy pants?

6. Suggest a possible title for the passage.

7. What size were Taiwo's pants?

RAIN AND ITS MEASUREMENT

A rain gauge is the <u>instrument</u> used for measuring rainfall. It has a metal cylinder with a glass jar inside, in which the rain that falls each day is collected. The rain water made to enter the glass jar through a funnel, in order to reduce evaporation. The rain gauge is <u>buried</u> in the ground with the top of the funnel about 30cm above the ground level. This is to prevent any rain <u>splashes</u> from the ground getting into the funnel.

The rain that falls into the glass jar is <u>emptied</u> every day and <u>measuredinmillimetres</u> in the measuring cylinder. This is a <u>calibrated</u> glass jar. The measuring jar is put on the palm and read at eye level. The monthly rainfall is got by adding together all the recorded readings for the days of the month. For the <u>annual</u> rainfall, the <u>readings</u> for twelve months of the year are added together.

QUESTIONS

1. Why does rain water enter the glass jar through a funnel?

2. What measure ensures that rain splashes from the ground do not enter the funny?

3. In one simple sentence, describe what a rain gauge is used for.

4. What is the unit for measuring rainfall?

5. What is done to the measuring jar before it is read?

The word calibrated used in the second paragraph means (a) to mark with units of measurement (b) to heat water (c) to increase temperature (d) to shake a cylinder

6. Evaporation is reduced by ______. (a) not allowing the glass jar into the rain gauge (b) heating up the cylinder (c) reducing the amount of water in the cylinder (d) making the rain water enter the glass jar through the funnel.

7. How many days make a monthly reading of the amount of rainfall? (a)15 (b) 20 (c) 30 (d) 25

8. What part of speech does the word "emptied" used in the second paragraph belong to? (a) noun (b) adjective (c) adverb (d) verb

9. The cylinder in which the jar is put is made of

(a) glass (b) plastic (c) metal (d) clay

TORTOISE; THE WISEST ANIMAL

A tortoise once promised to bring an elephant into town. Many people thought it was impossible for a small creature like the tortoise to lead an elephant into any town. But the tortoise fixed a date for this great event, and the king and all his people agreed to bargain, promising to pay the tortoise a large sum of money if he fulfilled his promise. But if he failed, he would be killed.

To prepare his plan, the tortoise dug a hole in the ground and covered it with a mat. He fried akara balls and went into the thick bush where the elephants generally lived. He was likely to meet the elephants who were holding an assembly. He addressed them and gave them some akara balls. They enjoyed the taste and desired more. Then the tortoise announced that he wanted to make one of the elephants a king and if anyone wished to eat more of the akara balls, he should follow him home because akara balls were special food of the kings. The youngest elephant, on hearing this, volunteered to follow him.

The elephant and the tortoise started their journey home. On the way, the tortoise continued to feed the elephant with akara balls. Every time he gave him one, he sang a song called: "This elephant will be crowned tomorrow."

A bird seeing the danger which the elephant would soon encounter sang to him that he would be killed the following day and his blood would be drunk by the people.

This elephant did not bother about the bird's song but continued to listen to the tortoise and to think of how he would enjoy being crowned. He followed the tortoise until they reached the big hole covered with a mat. The tortoise threw the akara balls to the elephant that fell into the pit while trying to catch them and there he died.

The tortoise collected the money which had been promised him and became very rich.

QUESTIONS

1. There are two settings to this story; what are they?

2. Why did the people doubt the promise of the tortoise to bring the elephant to town?

3. How did the tortoise arouse the youngest elephant's interest?

4. What was the bird's music to the elephant?

5. ... If he fulfilled his promise... what type of adverbial clause is this?

6. Why didn't the elephant give ear to the bird's music?

7. ...who were holding an assembly... what grammatical name is this? What is its function?

8. What killed the elephant?

9. What moral lesson did you learn from this story? State at least two.

MR.CISSEY

Mr. Cissey pulled on his trousers hurriedly and dragged himself to the verandah. He was bent on getting to his office before his workers. The previously day, he had <u>reprimanded</u> his staff for regularly coming to work late, and threatened to give the sack to any of them who would repeat the offence. Today, he must get to work in time not only to serve as a role model but also to show that he really meant what he had said.

He managed to squeeze behind the wheel of his car which was at least two sizes too small to accommodate his paunch. He inserted the ignition key and turned it but the car would not start; the engine just grumbled. On the second attempt, it coughed and finally roared to life on the third. It moved grudgingly to the gate and stopped. Cissey immediately realized that he would be caught in a traffic jam. It was <u>evident</u> that he would arrive at his workplace late.

For about two hours, Cissey sat, glued to his seat, fuming. Hard as he tried to control his temper, the misbehavior of other drivers once <u>prompted</u>

him to bawl at them. Then suddenly after the interminable wait, the street cleared and Cissey sped off. It was almost three hours after leaving home that he got to his workplace. The staff were already there and when he entered the building he found the secretary and the clerical staff apparently immersed in their assignments, with an air of dutifulness. One look at their boss warned them that they had better keep quiet to save their skin. But as soon as he closed the door to his office, he heard soft voices mumbling words he could not understand. Worst of all, he heard subdued laughter from his secretary.

Cissey immediately shot out of the chair ready to vent his spleen on these underlings but suddenly plopped back into his seat. On the second thoughts, he changed his mind. How could he castigatethem for what they had not caused?

QUESTIONS

1. Why was Mr. Cissey in a hurry to get to his office?

2. What two indications are there in the passage that Mr. Cissey was a huge man?

3. How did Mr. Cissey express his anger while caught in the traffic?

4. Why did Mr. Cissey become angry with his

staff?

5. What was the attitude of the staff towards their boss?

6. ... when he entered the building... what grammatical name is given to this expression as it is used in the passage? (b) What is its function?

7. *How could he castigate them for what they had not caused?* What literary device is used in this-expression?

8. What is meant by the expression *vent his spleen* in the last paragraph?

9. State the synonyms of the following words (i) prompted (ii) reprimanded (iii) evident (iv) immersed

THE GIRL THAT CANNOT CRY

'I am going to tell you a chilling story'. Do you see the scares on my face? They are marks of torture. I wasbeaten up by members of my extended family who insisted I was a witch and I should makea public confession. I wasn't a witch! I didn't even know what it meant to be a witch. I was only eight years old when the first attempt at extracting a confession from me was made. My favourite aunt had just died. Two days before, she had told me she was going on a long journey and she would not be coming back. I had asked her where she was going. She had replied "To Papa in heaven". In my childhood innocence, I had broadcast this to the hearing of everyone. So when she died the following day, it was presumed I must have killed her. I was taken to a native healer who tied me up and asked them to beat me up if I refused to confess and tell them the source of my powers. [They dug their fingers into my face and thrashed me with special whips provided by the healer.] "Not a drop of tears is coming from her eyes. Only witches don't cry" they added. I passed out and woke up in the hospital several days later. When my parents came to see me, they confirmed that I had always been stoned-hearted, never once shedding tears no matter how sad everyone. I was a mystery. I wish I can cry like most ofyou butnot a drop of tearshas ever come down my cheeks. I have paid for it different ways. My friend and classmates think I have no emotions and avoid me like the plague. My gap-tooth doesn't help matters too. People think I am smiling whenever I open my mouth. I have seen people cry for joy but for me no matter how charged the situation is, shedding tears is impossible.

'My doctor has tried to explain the reason why I have been unable to cry. He says, "There are three types of tears generated by the human eye. The Basal tears protect the eye and keep it moist. Reflect tears flush out the eye when it becomes irritated. Emotional tears are produced as a means of communication. It flows in response to sadness, distress or physical pain. There are many reasons for one's inability to cry." My doctor said in my own case the inability to cry may be caused by a rare genetic affliction. Even though I experience emotions like everyone else, I was born without the reflex necessary to produce tears.

QUESTIONS

1. In four sentences, one for each, state the different ways the speaker has suffered injustice as a result of her inability to cry.

2. In one sentence, state the possible cause of the speaker's inability to cry according to her doctor.

ABSURD

Once more, Jeri turned the bicycle upside down, spurns the wheels expertly, and listened with his palm over the back of his ear, absorbing every little sound that was out of tune. "That noise! It is still here", he muttered. "The crank wheel needs lubrication."

"Is Lu there? He called, still listening. When the boy came he sent him for oil-can. But a few moments later, Frank ran out with the can while Fred followed with a rag.

"Eyiii" Frank exclaimed pointing to the rotating wheels."Fred, see, see! The bicycle is dancing in the air."Not dancing, it's doing its own type of magic, "his brother corrected. They both moved forward to have a closer look. But he barred their approach with his hands. About a few years ago, one of the children –Lu it was!- had inserted a stick into the spokes as the wheel spun exactly like that, and he was forced to replace six spokes in a single day.

"Go back."

Frank proposed a deal: "Give us something if you want us to."

"Like."

The child laughed in anticipation. "Meat. Give the joint over the fireplace."

"That is not to be touched, he said and went on dropping oil into the recesses of the wheel. "I shall cook it for you if you happen to be sick."

I am now," Fred said, then coughed, "see?"

He laughed "Go and tell your mama, perhaps she will give you some of it."

In that way he got rid of them. He spun the back wheel once more, turning the pedal rod energetically. And then, it was launched into a continuous, fluid whirl, and the outlines disappeared completely. He brought his ear closer again, nodded with contentment and began to sing: "Guard, Kindly guard."

Questions

1. Why did Jeri turn the bicycle upside down?

2. What is the oil-can used for?

3. Why did Jeri disallow Frank and Fred from moving near the bicycle?

4. For how long had Jeri owned the bicycle?

5. What did Fred do hoping that Jeri wound believe he was not well?

6. For each of the following words find another word that means the same and can replace it as it is in the passage:

Expertly

Lubrication

Inserted

Proposed

Completely

Contentment

LOST IN THE FARM

There was a time I wronged my Uncle, my father's elder brother, who brought me up. On this occasion, my cousin and I had overstayed our specific time on the farm, causing the whole household a lot of <u>panic.</u> We had been instructed not to stay beyond late afternoon at the farm-land, no matter what work we might be doing on the farm. That day, because we were hunting small game, we forgot ourselves. Early afternoon grew into evening, then darkness was setting in. the farther into the bush we hunted the more game we caught. We were quite <u>oblivious</u> of the risks to which we exposed ourselves. Cases of child kidnapping were <u>rampant</u> then, though we had never had a brush with the child-hunting ritual killers. Suddenly, darkness descended like a dark curtain. It dawned on us that there was someone at home whose rules we had broken.

Quickly, we ran home but it was too late; the whole household had set out to look for us at the farmstead, which we had left hours earlier for the bush. Their panic had multiplied on their reaching the empty farmstead. Getting home, discovering that only old granny was in, we knew we had had it. Meanwhile, my uncle and his luckless team went from one farmstead to another searching for us. When it was too dark for them to find their way around, they bent their steps towards home to plan the next search strategy. But then they found us waiting.

The old man was too <u>fired</u>, too angry to beat us. He just stared like the devil at us. Oh! <u>How much that stare froze me!</u> Wished <u>I could just melt away before his eyes</u>. I wished he had taken a whip and <u>thrashed</u> me. But he didn't! he simply sat in that dark corner of the room, bent double like a tired masquerade. Looking at his _pathetic_ figure down there, I couldn't bear it any longer: I started crying it was then I discovered that my cousin had indeed set the pace, only that he had been sobbing quietly.

QUESTIONS

1. (i) What specific order had the writer and his cousin been given? (ii) What prevailing situation had warranted to this?

2, What had made the two forget the order?

(i) What did the writer expect from his uncle when the search party arrived? (ii) Why?

3. What caused the writer to cry?

"……………… I could just melt away before his eyes."

"How much that stare froze me?"

4. What figure of speech is used in the expression above?

  What does it mean?

5. For each of the following words, find another

word or phrase, which means the same, and which can replace it as it is used in the passage:

Panic

Oblivious

Rampant

Tired

Thrashed

Pathetic

EMERGENCY MEETING

'Gentlemen1' the Chairman called the meeting to order. 'I welcome you all to this important emergency meeting of the Provisional Council of this university...' He touched on some of the major setback which the university had encountered in recent times, mentioning particularly the students and the lecturers' strike and the dastardly acts of the cultists in which lethal weapons were freely used. The administration did not sit back and watch these unfortunate developments with folded arms. Although the Council had not met, the able Vice-Chancellor had been in intermittent consultation with him in an attempt to diagnose the problems and prescribe the most effective remedies. The Administration had now come up with series of proposals which would come before an ordinary meeting of the Council at a later date. The present emergency meeting was to consider one proposal only- the most crucial. Because of its high delicate and confidential nature of the proposal had not been circulated in writing to members before the meeting, as was the usual practice. He called on the Vice-Chancellor to table his proposal. The Vice-Chancellor then cleared his throat and commenced his speech.

'Respected Ladies and Gentlemen,' said the Vice Chancellor, 'we have a serious situation on our hands. A few cultists are out to destroy the good work which you and I have been doing in this noble university. That the cultists have killed and maimed several persons on campus is no longer news. The activities of the cultists have become a frightful monster staring all of us in the face. To avoid a situation of anarchy on campus therefore we are proposing that any cultist-be he a student or a member of staff-caught should not only be dismissed but also be made to face the full wrath of the law. In this case there will be no sacred cow. Even the child of the Vice-Chancellor or the Vice-Chancellor himself is apprehended as a cultist should be dealt with, in fact, more severely than others. Nobody, no matter how highly placed, should be allowed to disturb the peace, the tranquillity and the serenity for which this university is noted and of which we all are proud. Thank you.

QUESTIONS

1. What was the purpose of the emergency meeting of the University Council?

2. With whom had the Vice-Chancellor been in constant consultation?

3. What had the Administration done about the problems in the university before the meeting?

4. What was the proposal put forward by the Vice-Chancellor?

5. Why was the proposal not communicated to the members of the Council?

5. '... a frightful monster,' What figure of speech is that?

6. 'The present emergency meeting...'

What grammatical name is given to this expression?

What is its function?

7. For each of the following words, find another word or phrase that means the same and can replace it as it is used in the passage.

Lethal

Table

Anarchy

ORJI ONYEBUCHI

Practice

Commenced

Apprehended.

THE EYE

Seeing involves a number of processes. The image of the object viewed must first be formed on the retina. The stimulus of light reflected from the figure must then be received by the rods or cones, depending on the light intensity. Finally, the impulse of this stimulus must be transmitted through the optic lobe of the brain, which correctly interprets the image.

To form the image of an object on the retina, light rays from the object must pass through the conjunctiva, cornea, aqueous humour, lens and vitreous humour to the retina. All these parts are transparent and contribute to the refraction of light entering the eye, thus enabling the rays to converge at the retina. The image of the object formed on the retina is inverted and smaller than the object. However, the brain interprets size and orientation of the image correctly. In order to form a sharp image of an object, all the light rays reflect from a particular point on it must meet again exactly at a point on the retina. The image of the object will be blurred.

Have you noticed that after you have been reading a book continuously for hours, your eyes require a short period of adjustment to be able to see a distant figure clearly again? This adjustment of the eyes to a new situation is known as accommodation. Accommodation is the adjustment of the eyes in order to bring an image into focus. When viewing a distant object, the shape of the lens of the eyes is always thinner and longer than when viewing a near object. On the other hand, to bring a near object to focus, the lens of the eye becomes more thickened and rounded like a ball.

QUESTIONS

1. What is this passage all about

2. What is the function of the optic lobe?

3. Mention what the following have in common- conjunctiva, cornea, lens and vitreous humour.

4. State the importance of accommodation.

5. 'In order to form a sharp image of an object...' (i) What grammatical name is given to this expression? (1mk) (ii) what is its function?

6. '... Like a ball.' What figure of speech is used in the above expression?

    b. what is the meaning?

7. For each of the following words, find another word or phrase that means the same and can replace it as it is used in the passage.

Intensity (ii) transmitted (iii) converge (iv) require (v) blurred

WHAT THEY THINK

What do young people usually think of? A recent study has revealed that young people, boys and girls, in the primary schools are often preoccupied with problems usually associated with adults. Contrary to what most of us would have expected, it was found that these young people are already bothered by issues such as what kind of husband or wife they would marry; what profession they would prefer; the type of car they would drive, and how they would cope with the scarcity of money. Surprisingly, most of them are <u>scared</u> by prospects of marital problems, and some take it for granted that divorce is the way out of difficult marriages.

However, it is most surprising that political issues rarely feature among the problems bothering them. They seem to be hardly preoccupied with the thought of who governs them, the kind of government in the country or its political ideology. Nonetheless, quite a good number of them are serious. Beyond this, <u>what they would do afterwards</u> does not seem to <u>con-</u>

<u>cern</u> them nor can they define precisely how they would attain these positions.

It appears that children's thought patterns are shaped or, at least, influenced by the environment within which they live. For instance, while most of those from happily married parents think of the kind of spouse to marry, those from polygamous or broken homes tend to envisage marital problems and divorce. Again, children from <u>humble</u> backgrounds, for example, where the parents are farmers, carpenters, mechanics and those from rural or semi-urban areas are less ambitious. They usually opt for more conventional <u>professions</u> like teaching and nursing. On the other hand, children from more sophisticated backgrounds tend to opt for less conventional profession such as aeronautical engineering, accountancy and banking.

From all that has been discussed so far, an obvious lesson is that children should not be exposed to unhealthy ideas and unpleasant thoughts as their aspirations and actions are indeed influenced by their environment.

QUESTIONS

1. What is the purpose of the opening question in the passage?

2. How did the writer obtain the information contained in this passage?

3. What does the author find surprising about young people's thought patterns as contained in the first paragraph?

4. What effect does parents' marital experience have on their children's ideas about marriage?

5. What does the passage say about children's attitude to politics?

6. Who generally influences children in forming their opinion?

7. .... What they would do afterwards........................." what grammatical name is given to this expression? What is its function?

8. For each of the following words, find another word or phrase, which can replace it as it is used in the passages:

    Revealed

    Scared

    Concern

    Spouse

Humble

NIGERIA PALM OIL

About thirty years ago, Nigeria was a large exporter of palm oil and had been for many years before then. You have probably read about the oil rivers of the last century. Well, they were not so-called because they were oil rigs dotted around them as now, but because of the export of palm oil from the region.

Palm oil is also very important to us at home as we use it a great deal in our cooking. Some of you may like groundnut oil soup better, but it is not as good for you as palm oil. Palm oil is rich in vitamins A and D and helps to protect us from diseases. So isn't it a pity that today we have become importers of palm oil instead of exporters?

There are many reasons for this. First, the civil war destroyed many oil farms in the area where it was the main livelihood of the people. The south of our countries is a natural home for palm trees, having the right conditions, a hot humid climate and rich soil. Then the petroleum boom in the country hit like a cyclone. It had a devastating effect on the palm oil industrial as upon agriculture in general. In a get- rich-quick rush to the urban centres by people looking for jobs in the new industries and factories, young men forgot all about harvesting the oil palms: there was easier money to be picked up and an exciting city life as well.

As a result people like me who had modest oil palm farms in the south had the heart-break of being unable to keep their farms weeded, let alone get the nuts harvested.

So it was gradually, or not so gradually, we became importers instead of exporters of palm oil. For some years now, successive Federal Governments have been worried about this. They have realised that it is essential to revive this vital industry so that instead of costing us precious foreign exchange, palm oil can earn us a little more of those much-needed currencies-provided we produced high quality oil in sufficient quantity.

The five hundred million naira that the Federal Government has injected into the industry in an effort to reactivate it should prove an effective shot in the arm. As well as opening a seven hundred-million-naira Federal Palm Oil Mill at ElereAdubi in Ifo Ota, the Federal Government is urging the private sector industrialists to go into oil palm planting and processing. In adding, in order to ensure that seedlings are available to prospective farmers, it has also directed each state Ministry of Agriculture to set up an extension service board. Finally, local farmers are being encouraged to intensify the harvesting oil palm produce and to establish new oil palm farms to make sure that the new mill has a regular and sufficient supply of raw materials.

QUESTIONS

(a) State in three sentences, one for each, the three reasons that the writer gives for the decline of the oil palm industry.

(b) In two sentences, one for each, state the two steps the Federal Government has taken to revive the oil palm industry.

THE MAGICIAN

The chanters emerged from the doorway. In their midst was the fire walker, his eyes <u>focused on</u> the ground. He was like a <u>man eroded of his will</u>, captured by the band of chanters. They walked towards the fire which was now a glowing mass of flames leaping <u>here and there.</u>

The chanters grouped themselves near the fire and went on with their singing and bell-ringing, shouting refrains energetically. Then, <u>as though life had suddenly flowed into him,</u> the fire-walker removed himself from the group and went towards the fire. It was a tense moment. The chanters were <u>gripped</u> by frenzy. The coal-bed glowed. He placed his right foot on the fire gently, tentatively, as though measuring its intensity, and then walked swiftly over from end to end. He was <u>applauded</u>. Two boys now offered him coconuts in trays. He <u>selected</u> two, and then walked over the inferno again, rather slowly this time, and<u> as he walked</u>, he banged the coconuts against his head several times until they cracked and one saw the snowy insides. His movement now became more like a dance than a walk, as though his feet gloried in their <u>triumph</u> over the fire. The boys offered him more coconuts and he went on breaking them against his head.

QUESTIONS

1. According to the passage, who is the fire-walker?

2. was the fire-walker eyes focused on the ground?

3. What does the writer mean by "a man eroded of his own will?"

4. What figure of speech is exemplified by the clause" as though life had suddenly flowed into him?"

5. Give for each of the following a word or phrase that could take its place in the passage:

Focused on (ii) applauded (iii) triumph (iv) here and there (v) gripped (vi) selected (vii) triumph

FAILED AMULETS

Dele groaned and got out of bed. There was no clock on the mantel piece and the room was still dark, but he knew he was already late for work, probably by up to an hour, he was a commercial bus driver and had to get started as early as 5. 00a.m and go almost non-stop until about 9.00p.m. to be able to make the daily returns that the bus owner demanded.

On the previous day, he had attended an all-night party- a late uncle's burial ceremony- where he had drunk himself almost senseless before crawling home in the early hours of the morning. Now he got up shakily, splashed water on his face and hurried off to work, but not before carefully fastening on his upper left arm the amulet he had always worn for protection against accident. A similar amulet hung concealed under the steering column of his bus. On his way, still feeling groggy, he caught his left toe against a stump and had some misgiving. It was a bad sign, and he was supposed to go back home and then set out again. But there was no time for that now, so he hurried on.

At the bus station, Dele quickly loaded his bus and sped off without any necessary checks on the vehicle. He had to make up for lost time. It was the rush hour, so the bus was overloaded as it often was, with many passengers hanging on to the doors. The tyres were threadbare, the brakes were faulty and the road was wet, but, still feeling a little sleepy, Dele sped on. Many passengers protested against his reckless driving, but he would not listen. After all, didn't he have protection against accident?

As the vehicle took the last turn before its destination, Dele saw a broken-down truck blocking his side of the road. Under normal circumstances, he could have brought the bus safely to a halt, but the circumstances were far from normal. The careering bus hit the parked vehicle, swerved wildly across the road and plunged into a ditch.

Dele's surprise before he sank into oblivion was the failure of his supposedly protective amulets.

QUESTIONS

1. Why did Dele wake up late?

2. '...he caught his left toe against a stump and had some misgiving.' What does this tell us

about Dele?

3. Give two reasons why Dele drove recklessly.

4. Why was Dele unable to stop his faulty vehicle?

5. What was Dele's condition after the accident?

6. 'After all, didn't he have protection against accident?' what literary device is used in this expression?

7. '...wildly across the road...' (i) What is the grammatical name given to this expression as it is used in the passage? (ii) what is its function?

CONTAINER LORRIES

It is now a common sight to see container lorries moving equipment and goods from one place to another. Has anyone bothered to think about the dangers posed by these containers? Have those at the helms of affairs given any thought to reviving the rail transport which has been "killed" for selfish reasons? Have they thought about the advantages of rail transport over haulage by container lorries?

One of the dangers posed by these container lorries is the destruction of telephone and electricity wires thus disrupting the communication system and hampering services of the Power Holding Company. More often than not, the container lorries, in an attempt to move goods from place to place, because of their great height, damage electricity wire and thus throw whole communities or villages or even towns into darkness.

I once witnessed an incident, which is a common occurrence, in which a container turned over on top of a car. It was quite a sorry sight.

The car was damaged beyond repairs. There was only one survivor out of the four occupants of the car.

What about the roads on which the container Lorries travel? The container Lorries, because of their weight, frequently damage portions of the roads on which they travel. Do the drivers or the owners of the container Lorries bother about the damages? No, they are not concerned about the damage done. Unfortunately, the members of the public are made to bear the burden of effecting repairs on the roads. How? By using the tax-payers' money for the repairs. Thus, the tax payer is made to be responsible for destruction about which they know nothing. Is it fair?

The drivers of the container Lorries regard their vehicles as 'king of the road' and so they drive with reckless abandon. They harass and intimidate other road users. The hooting of their horns alone is enough to frighten other road users out of their wits. There was one incident I witnessed in which a car owner, having been harassed, swerved off the road and landed into a ditch.

In contrast, rail transport is much better and safer too. One of the point in favour of reviving the rail transport is the fact that it is cheaper to move goods and equipment than these dangers on the roads referred to as container lorries. The effect it will have is that the prices of goods and equipment will decrease, since the consumer is made to bear the cost of transportation (no matter how high) of the goods purchased.

Also the lives of innocent people- car-owners or even pedestrians are not endangered by the use of rail transport as is often the case with container lorries.

QUESTIONS

1. In three sentences, one for each, state three disadvantages of using container lorries in the haulage industry

2. In two sentences, one for each, state two advantages of using the rail transport in moving goods and equipment from one place to another.

POPULATION EXPLOSION IN THE SEA

Tortevieja, a tourist centre recorded the highest number of visitors during the last summer. About 600,000 people visited the centre because of the bright weather. The councillor for tourism reported that all the hotels were fully occupied and so were the cafeterias and restaurants. Despite the avalanche (large number) of visitors, electricity and drinking water were in regular supply. But there were transport problems especially on the roads where traffic jams had been overwhelming and parking places inadequate.

The new comers, visitors and residents continued to enjoy the last few weeks of summer, but the hot days and long night were not good news for everyone. Experts warned that the rise in temperature was a threat to fish population because of the heating up of the Mediterranean Sea which in July was in 6 degrees above average. They warned also that the fishing resources were in danger as the ecosystems were altered. This, they claimed would lead to the disappearance of fish and crustaceans of commercial interest.

The heating up of the sea bed affected numerous species. Those that could not tolerate the heat moved to colder waters, while other species from warmer habitats moved to a more adequate habitat.

Among the tropical fish which arrived through the straits of Gibraltar and the Suez Canal were "Moray and Conger eels, large crabs and species of shark. However, the increased temperature resulted in the explosion in the population of jellyfish encouraged by the increased currents.

This shows that it is not only human being that are affected by high population, sea animals too are increasing at an alarming rate.

QUESTIONS

1. hy were tourists at the tourist centre?

2. Two basic features function well; what are they?

3. Why do experts fear the increase in the temperature at the sea?

4. What happen to the fish that could not tolerate the heat at the sea?

5. How many sharks were found on the beaches?

6. ....a tourist centres... what grammatical name is this?

   What is its function?

7. Write the synonym of the following (i) explosion (ii) threat (iii) avalanche

8. Where can we find the largest of fishes in the world? What are they used for?

MYSTERIES OF NUMBERS

Imagine a world without numbers. There would be no money. Trade would be restricted to face-to-face barter. And what about sports? Without numbers, not only would we be unable to keep score but we could not even define how many players should be on each team!

Besides their practical application, however, numbers carry an <u>aura of mystery</u>. This is because they are abstract. You cannot see, touch, or feel numbers. To illustrate: An apple has a distinct colour, texture, size, shape, small, and taste. You can check each of these properties to see whether a certain object is indeed an apple, a lemon, a ball, or something else. A number, however, is not like that. One collection of seven items may not share anything in common with another collection of seven items–other than their "sevenness". Hence, to comprehend the meaning of number - for example, to discern the difference between six and seven- is to grasp something very abstract indeed. And this is where number mystics come into the picture.

From Pythagoras to Pseudoscience

Attributing special meaning to numbers was common in ancient societies. Pythagoras, a Greek philosopher and mathematician <u>who lived during the sixth century</u>, taught that all things can be reduced to numerical patterns. He and his followers reasoned that the whole universe exemplifies order and proportion–could it not be, then that mathematical relationships are inherent in all materials things?

Questions

1. State the two immediate problems likely to be faced by a world without numbers

2. Explain the phrase "aura of mystery"

3. What gives this feature to number?

4. What are the things you cannot do with numbers?

5. Name the physical features of an apple?

6. What does the author call these features?

7. Why are these features relevant in the relationship between an apple and numbers?

8. What was common in ancient societies?

9. ...'who lived during the sixth century' what grammatical name is this? ii. What is its function?

10. What was the ultimate reasoning of Pythagoras and his followers?

ADULTHOOD

To define who an adult is may be <u>a herculean task</u>, for each society has its <u>criteria</u> for determining who an adult is. Among the <u>parameters</u> is chronological age. Here, the number of years an individual has lived on earth is used as a <u>determinant</u> of whether he is an adult or not. But it has been proved that an older person may not always be wise and a child who is knowledgeable say in the field of history could be more effective in recounting past events than an adult. We may say that an adult is one who biologically has his five senses functioning. Yet it has been discovered that the effectiveness of the biological system of the body depends on the standard of living of individual adult. An individual <u>who lives a very healthy and qualitative life</u> is likely to live for a longer time before experiencing the physiological <u>depreciation</u> of his organs than someone whose quality of life is low. Again, an adult is not a person who is able to live up to the expectation of his society by the different roles he plays, nor can we accept the political concept of attainment of economics status, as being of <u>empirical</u> standing. Psychologically, an individual who cannot combine the use of the three domains of cognitive, affective and psychomotor and manifest mature behavior cannot be regarded as an adult.

An adult <u>succinctly</u> described by Paulo Freire as a 'person with considerable experience of living' and is therefore not an empty head. An adult is a person who has come to appreciate freedom and cherish it without being dehumanized

QUESTIONS

1. Why does the writer consider the definition of an adult the herculean task?

2. What argument is used to debunk the use of chronological age to determine who an adult is?

3. List three of the criteria mentioned in the passage used in attempting to define who an adult is?

4. Psychologically, how can a person be considered an adult?

5. '...who lives a very healthy and qualitative life?' What is the grammatical name given to the above expression?

6. What is its function in the sentence?

'... a herculean task'.

7. What figure of speech is the above expression? What does it mean?

8. For each of the following words, find another word or phrase that means the same and can replace it as it is used in the passage
I. Criteria (ii parameters (iii) determinant (iv) depreciation (v) empirical (vi) succinctly

HONESTY

Mr. Abu left home this morning in a sad mood. He had told his wife he was going to work. Suddenly, he came across a big brown envelope. He picked it up, open it and found several items inside. He brought out a passport belonging to Chu Lin, a Chinese national. He brought out an identity card: also, Chu Lin's – a staff of a multinational company which runs a chain of hotels in Lagos. There was a smaller envelope. He opened this as well. To his surprise, he discovered fifty thousand dollars in it.

Just this morning, Mr. Abu had been called a never-do-well. Their little boy James, was very ill and there was no money to take him to private hospital and the doctors in the state hospital are on strike. Mr. Abu's wife had called him an irresponsible man who is incapable of adequately providing for his family. She assumed that he squanders his salary. If only she knew the whole truth. In fact, Mr. Abu left home that morning as always to avoid his wife's constant nagging. He lost his job a few months back when the company he worked for folded up. Moreover, the company had not fulfilled its promise to pay Mr. Abu and his retrenched colleagues their severance pay. Mr. Abu was at his wits' end. He was also afraid that he might lose little James, his only son.

Mr. Abu's mind raced. He thought of all that he could do with just one thousand dollars. Perhaps he could take just that and drop the envelope. "No I will not do that", he said to himself. He checked the address on Chu Lin's identity card and headed for the company. It was a seven a kilometer trek.

On getting there, Mr. Abu asked to see Chin Lin. When he came out, Abu checked the identity card to ensure that he was with the right person. Satisfied, he handed Chu Lin the envelope without saying a word. Chu Lin didn't know whether to laugh or cry. He thought he had lost the envelope for good. He was full of gratitude. He wanted to give Mr. Abu some money but Mr. Abu would have none of it. Instead, he asked for a job. Chu Lin listened to his story. Immediately, Mr. Abu was given a job as a front desk officer in one of the company's hotels. 'We need honest people like you in that position,' Chu Lin said. Not only that, he gave Mr. Abu fifty thousand naira to settle his immediate family problems. Honesty pays after all.

QUESTIONS

1. In three sentences, one for each, state three reasons why Mr. Abu could have taken one thousand dollars from Chin Lin's money.

2. In two sentences, one for each, state two ways in which Mr. Abu was rewarded for his honesty.

FORCE MARRIAGE

'They, my father and my mother, gave me to your father at Idasa. I did not question their authority. I did not question their wisdom. I married your father. I lived with him till ... 'Here, she broke down overwhelmed by some painful recollection.

'Look at me Toro. Listen to me, Toro, I gave birth to you as my mother as given birth to me. And as my mother and my father gave me to your father in marriage, so, I, too, with the <u>consent</u> of your father's people, gave you to Tokunbo. I have not committed a crime in bearing you as my daughter. Others have three or four daughters. These daughters always marry whoever their mothers choose for them. 'Tokunbo is a worthy man, Toro. Tokunbo is a wealthy man. He is strong. He <u>descends</u> from a line of kings and warriors. His father remains a legend in the annals of tribe. He is very good looking. Toro, all the young women in the village feel flattered <u>whenever he greets them</u>. You must marry Tokunbo, my child.

Toro, you must heed my words', she said rather

fiercely. Toro, you must heed my words. Toro, I enjoin you to marry Tokunbo. By great travail I underwent at your birth, by bush tracks that I trudged to the native doctors' hamlets when you lay between life and death, in the name of womanhood I command you to marry Tokunbo.

She paused for a long while after this, she coughed. It was a big burden off her chest. Then she asked: 'you will marry Tokunbo, Toro?' No answer. 'You will marry Tokunbo, won't you Toro? Two streams rolled down the girl's cheeks. 'You will marry Tokunbo Toro, or else you will face the consequences, Toro'. She said fiercely.

The consequences of refusing to marry Tokunbo, the girl knew what they were. Parents could exercise the ancient right of giving a dis-obedient daughter to the Oba as a gift bride. A daughter who refused to marry the suitor of her parents' choice was invariably sent to the Oba's palace. There she regretted her <u>folly</u> at leisure. She would become one of the many wives of Oba. A new member of the large harem, she would be attached as a ward to an elderly wife; for whom she would <u>slave</u> as domestic servant while she learnt in return the endless tradition, rites and life in the palace.

QUESTIONS

1. 'I did not question their authority'. By using the word 'their', who is the speaker referring to?

2. Why in your opinion, did the speaker need the consent of the family of Toro's father before giving her to Tokunbo in marriage?

3. What would be the consequences of Toro refusing to marry Tokunbo?

4. Describe the atmosphere in the passage. What is the tone of Toro's mother's speech?

5. Do you think Toro wants the marriage? Support your answer with quotes from the passage.

6. …for whom she would slave as a domestic servant… what part of speech is the word 'slave' in the quotation?

7. …whenever he greets them. What grammatical name is given to this expression? (ii) What is its function?

8. For each of the following words, find another words or phrase which means the same and can replace it as it is used the passage. (i) Consent (ii) folly (iii) suckled (iv) entreat

SILENT KILLER

The morning I woke up not knowing where I was, convinced me that something was terribly wrong. That was eight months ago. Now I know that my 10-year old daughter Sophie and I had been slowly poisoned by carbon monoxide leaking from a faulty gas fire in our front room. Everything was fine until a year after the new gas fire was installed. I began to forget things. I'd go to the shops and couldn't remember what I'd gone for, while paying bills just slipped my mind. I felt really tired-I'd have to fight to keep my eyes open and stop my legs buckling beneath me. I began to struggle at work. My doctor diagnosed depression but the medication he prescribed made no difference, nothing worked. I was argumentative and nasty, and would shout and scream at people. My mother would come to see me and I'd yell at her to get out.

She thought I was mad. Sophie struggled at school too. She couldn't concentrate and would end up fidgeting or throwing a tantrum. The breakthrough came last November when my neighbor told me she'd called in an engineer to check a smell of gas in her home. After investigating it, he said it was coming from my house and told me to get checked for carbon monoxide poisoning.

QUESTIONS

1. In three sentences one for each, state the symptoms of carbon monoxide poisoning as experienced by the writer.

2. In one sentence, state the effect of this poisoning on her daughter, Sophie.

3. In one sentence state the source of this poisoning.

ROAD ACCIDENT

We are interested in the various kinds of injury that can occur in road traffic accidents, how to prevent them and their first aid management. Most of us have probably witnessed one form of road traffic accident or another. The universal reaction of eye-witnesses is panic as they rush to the scene and there stand there looking in dismay. Road traffic accidents are great crowd – pullers as everyone wants to stop and have a look. However, the three most useful things you can do if you are at the scene of a road traffic accident are to assist in the rescue of the trapped victims; to render first aid treatment to victims; and to help in conveying injured people to the nearest hospital.

Road traffic accidents have a great potential for causing injury to the human body. The high velocity at which the most vehicles is travelling the sudden acceleration impact and the hard rigid nature of the motor-car body, all contribute to increase the potentials of injury, probably, the most risk-laden road traffic accidents are those which involve motor-cyclists as they do not have a solid motor-car body to protect them from the direct impact of an oncoming vehicle on the road. Road traffic accidents involving motor-cyclists are the cause of high mortality as the human skull is often fractured on impact with the hard surface of the road.

Road traffic accidents involving cars and their passages can cause some serious problems as the wreckage of the car may trap some people inside. This may mean that the crumpled car body needs to be cut away before the victims can be saved. If the road accident results in a fire, then this can be disastrous as the fire will prevent rescuers from coming near, thus resulting in the quick demise of the victim from burns. This is why every car-driver must possess a fire extinguisher in his vehicle. This little device may save in some situations.

QUESTIONS

1. What according to the writer, do eye –witnesses usually do as an accident occurs?

2. What three things does he suggest that eye-witnesses should do?

3. Mention two of the fact that can increase injuries during road accidents?

4. Why are motor-cyclists more at risk when accidents occur?

5. Why does the writer suggest that every car-driver should have a fire extinguisher in his vehicle?

5. *If the road accident result in a fire*

What is the grammatical name given to the above expression?

6. For each of following words, find another word or phrase that means the same and can replace it as it is used in the passage.

Universal;

Conveying;

Potentials;

Disastrous

NIGHT HUNTER

That evening, Musa Yakubu found the silence intolerable. His wife and his children had travelled to another village where they would spend the night. In Musa's hut, no child snored. No suckling wailed in demand for milk. No lamp burnt. Once in the house, Musa searched around for matches. He stumbled on a chair and fell. He tiptoed to the kitchen <u>where he sought but found no matches</u>. He entered his bed room, found his torchlight on his bed and return to the kitchen. He overturned the place in a futile search for a lamp and a box of matches.

Musa felt very angry. He dashed again into his bedroom, picked his gun, and locked the door behind him. He would go hunting. Night was the time to find antelopes and deer anyway. He proudly recalled the day he had killed a leopard. He also re-called the night before his father's burial rites when he had killed seven animals. Hunting was a productive way to spend <u>a barren night</u>

Once in the wilderness, however, Musa wondered if he had not taken a precipitate step. The games were not out. The batteries of his torch seemed to be running down. But Musa was not a person to <u>retreat</u> once he had taken a first step. He <u>advanced</u> further and further into the forest in the hope of being able to return home with at least a catch. The terrible thing was that there was no sign of an animal. Only squirrels <u>periodically</u> rattled the dry leaves on the ground, but he had no use for rodents. He matched on, stopping at <u>intervals</u> to listen, flashing his torchlight around.

He had almost given up hope when he heard footsteps from afar. He stopped. He was convinced that it was antelope.

The footsteps drew closer. The hunter switched off his torch. He fell on his knees and pointed his gun in the direction of the <u>approaching</u> steps. He fired. A loud human wail followed the shots

QUESTIONS

1. Why did Musa go hunting?

2. Write the three things Musa did before shooting. …a barren night…. What figure of speech is employed here?

3. What do you think Musa shot? How do you know?

4. … where he sought but found no food. What grammatical name is given to this expression (ii) what is its function

5. For each of following words, find another word or phrase that means the same and can replace it as it is used in the passage. (i) Retreat (ii) advanced (iii) periodically (iv) intervals (v) approaching

HUMAN ADVANCEMENT

Man did not stop his invention on communication with the radio and television. How about man-to-man communication? The telephone caters for this need, it has developed from the initial process of installing aerial wing or underground cables from one town to the other, to a completely wireless facility that can be kept in the breast pocket by men.

Man's curiosity to land on the moon has produced many bye-products, one of which is the use of the satellite for communication technology. The GSM mobile phone would not have come into existence but for the use of satellite for communication purposes

The greatest of them all at the moment is the computer. There is no doubt that man has not come to the end of the exploits in the use of the computer. Electronic mail can now be sent to the whole world within a second through the computer internet facilities. Individuals, companies, corporate bodies, states and countries now give volumes of information about themselves to the entire world through their established websites on the internet.

It is fashionable these days to see youth struggling in cyber cafes to get hold of a cubicle where they could do some internet browsing or send e-mails to their friends. A great deal of opportunities for educational advancement, scholarships, conferences, jobs and business are advertised on the internet. Honestly, the gains of the present day communication or information technological advancement are yet to be fully tapped by man.

QUESTIONS

1. Why did man not stop his intention on communication with the radio and television?

2. What was the initial process of making the telephone facility available?

3. How did the satellite come into communication technology?

4. Would you agree that the satellite gave birth to the GSM phone? Explain

5. xplain what you think people go for when they go for internet browsing

6. Summarize the last two paragraphs in two sentences each.

THE OSTRICH

Among the giraffes, zebra and gazelles that roam the _vast_ African savanna, perhaps the most _remarkable_ creature is the ostrich. Standing about 2.5 metres tall and weighing up to 155 kilograms, the ostrich is the largest bird in existence. No one can fail to be awed and _fascinated_ by the bird's great height, powerful legs and beautiful fluffy feathers.

Like the camel, the ostrich tolerant of high temperatures and _thrives_ in desert country. It also has long luxuriant eyelashes which protect its large eyes from the dust of the. Its legs are long and sinewy and its feet are strong and flashy. Seeing the ostrich strutting about in the open plains, observers are amazed, feeding on almost anything that creeps or crawls. It also dines on insects, snakes, rodents, roots and most vegetation. Because of its great size and weight, it cannot fly. However, its muscular legs are powerful enough to make it one of the fastest creatures on earth. Running across desert country, it can attain speeds of up to 65 kilometres an hour! This extraordinary swiftness and its long-distance stamina enable it to <u>outrun</u> many of the fastest four-legged predators with ease.

<u>The eggs of the ostrich</u> are the largest in the world can weigh up to 1.5 kilograms each. Prized for its size and delicious taste, each egg is the equivalent of 25 hens' eggs. The shell is hard and glossy and has a glazed porcelain-like finish. The empty shell is sometimes used as a container by bush men for storing water.

In the 14th century, ostrich feathers became highly valued by fashion conscious Europeans. Yet, hunting the ostrich was not easy, since the bird has very keen eyesight and swiftly flees from danger. Consequently, the ostrich was in no danger of <u>extinction</u> at that time.

But in the 19th century, armed with modern weapons, hunters slaughtered ostriches by the millions. And today the noble ostrich has become an endangered species.

QUESTIONS

1. Give three reasons why the ostrich egg is considered valuable

2. How does the ostrich survive attacj by predators?

3. What common characteristic of birds does the

ostrich lack?

4. Why did the Europeans value ostrich feathers?

5. "The eggs of the ostrich..."

What is the grammatical name given to this expression? What is its function as it is used in the passage?

What is the writer's attitude to the ostrich?

6. For each of the following words, find another word or phrase that mean the same and can replace it as it is used in the passage: (i) vast (ii) remarkable (iii) fascinated (iv) thrives (v) outrun (vi) extinction